CW00694485

NORFOLK
FROM THE AIR 2
A-Z

NORFOLK
FROM THE AIR 2
A-Z

MIKE PAGE & PAULINE YOUNG

HALSGROVE

First published in Great Britain in 2011

Copyright © photographs 2011 Mike Page
Copyright © text 2011 Pauline Young

All rights reserved. No part of this publication may be reproduced,
stored in a retrieval system, or transmitted in any form or by any
means without the prior permission of the copyright holder.

British Library Cataloguing-in-Publication Data
A CIP record for this title is available from the British Library

ISBN 978 0 85704 108 1

HALSGROVE
Halsgrove House,
Ryelands Business Park,
Bagley Road, Wellington, Somerset TA21 9PZ
Tel: 01823 653777   Fax: 01823 216796
email: sales@halsgrove.com

Part of the Halsgrove group of companies
Information on all Halsgrove titles is available at: www.halsgrove.com

Printed in China by Everbest Printing Co Ltd

This book is dedicated to the memory of
JAMES HOSEASON OBE 1927–2009

ACKNOWLEDGEMENTS

Mike Page wishes to thank Dan Gay, Graham Wright, Tim Ball, Brian Barr, Peter Day & Jonathan Howes for their co piloting assistance.

Pauline Young wishes to thank Huby Fairhead of the Norfolk and Suffolk Aviation Museum, Gary Kay, Patrick Lee, Judy Speed, Philip Warde and Brigadier A A Wilson OBE. And also our long suffering spouses Gillian Page and John Young for their tolerance and good humour during the preparation of this and our previous books.

INTRODUCTION

Since the publication of the first 'Norfolk from the Air' we have been saddened by the death of James Hoseason OBE. Jim was a good friend to so many both from within and outside East Anglia. A Suffolk man by birth his concerns for the region as a whole were evident in everything he undertook both in business and on a voluntary basis. His intelligent commonsense approach to matters both great and small and his many kindnesses are missed by all who knew him.

This second book of Norfolk from the Air contains both a catalogue of new places and records the progress of ongoing projects such as the development of Great Yarmouth's outer harbour, Sheringham Shoal Windfarm and Wells new harbour. Spectacular changes such as the rejoining of the railway line linking the Main Line with the Poppy Line at Sheringham and the start up of a significant new business at the Palm Paper plant on the site of the former Sugar Beet Processing factory at Kings Lynn are pictured within these pages. And familiar places such as the Floranova trial grounds and the Caister dig are shown from angles generally not seen.

One of Jim Hoseason's many achievements was the creation of the Waveney Flying Group at the former WW2 Seething Airfield. Without the Flying Group, of which we are both members, this series of eight books, might never have been written.

Mike Page
Strumpshaw

Pauline Young
Wymondham

Norfolk Coast and County

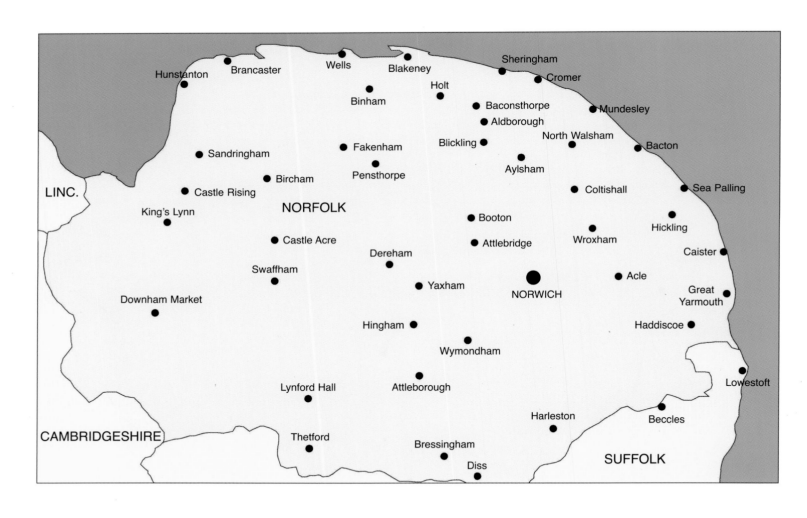

LINC.

Hunstanton
Brancaster
Wells
Blakeney
Sheringham
Cromer
Holt
Binham
Baconsthorpe
Mundesley
Aldborough
North Walsham
Bacton
Sandringham
Fakenham
Blickling
Bircham
Aylsham
Sea Palling
Castle Rising
Pensthorpe
NORFOLK
Coltishall
King's Lynn
Booton
Hickling
Castle Acre
Attlebridge
Wroxham
Dereham
Caister
Swaffham
Acle
Yaxham
NORWICH
Great
Downham Market
Yarmouth
Haddiscoe
Hingham
Lowestoft
Wymondham
Lynford Hall
Attleborough
Harleston
Beccles
CAMBRIDGESHIRE
Thetford
Bressingham
SUFFOLK
Diss

APACHE OVER NORFOLK
But not on a scalping mission!

SOUTHWARDS ON THE A11

Although this picture was taken only six miles from Norwich city centre the view is predominantly agricultural and remains so for the entire length of the county. The route southwards passes first through land composed of heavy clay soils which, on approaching Breckland, become light and sandy heathlands. Thankfully Wymondham (background) is now bypassed by this most recent A11 route; originally the London Road ran right through the middle of the town.

Right:
AERIAL ACROBATICS

August 2003 above the Norfolk countryside, preparing for a local air display.

FROM ACLE TO THE SEA

The River Bure divides the arable land from the marshes which extend to Breydon Water. Acle stands on the (slightly) higher ground which is apparent when approaching the village along the 'Acle Straight' (the A47) from Great Yarmouth. The railway and the A47 trunk road run parallel all the way to Yarmouth. In June when this picture was taken the bright yellow fields of rape seed grown for oil, cattle feed and biodiesel brighten the scene. But pollen from rape flowers reduces hay fever sufferers to tears. The Rivers Bure at the eastern end and the Yare and Waveney at the western end all flow into Breydon Water and thence out to sea.

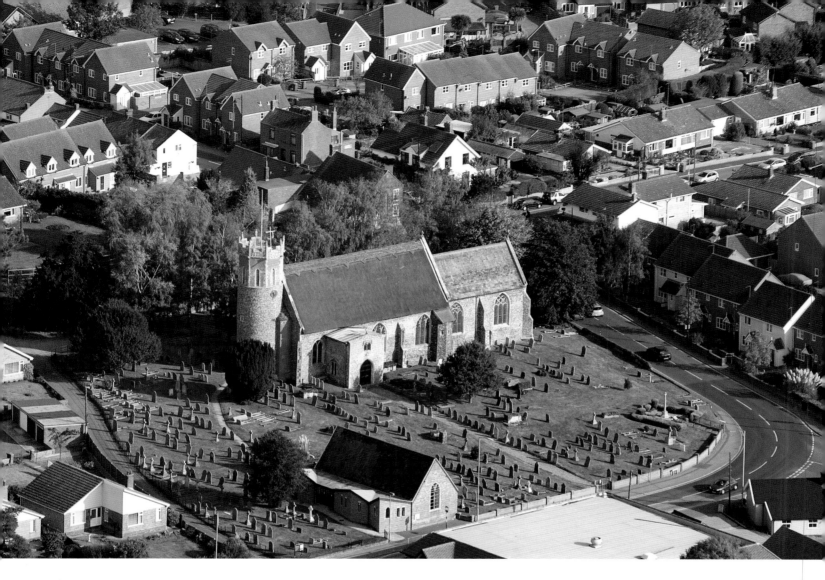

ACLE CHURCH

The Saxon round tower of St Edmund's church was built probably AD900. The octagonal stage was added probably in the 13th century and, according to the Church Reeve's Commonplace Book, the battlements were added in 1472 and cost £16. St Edmund's statue stands on the battlements facing towards his palace at Reedham. Edmund was King of East Anglia AD85-870. A scratch dial, forerunner of the sundial, is at head height on the south porch. There's an absence of old houses to the south of the church because the marshy land was deemed unsuitable for building. To put a bypass round the village it was necessary to pile the ground through a considerable depth of peat. The church hall was paid for by the Great Eastern Railway Company because the company's track runs across church land. On the land to the east of the church, where once a manor house stood, excavations into a 12th century midden are ongoing today.

13

ARMINGHALL VILLAGE

Beyond the mist lies Norwich. Around 3000BC a wood henge, a prehistoric site of worship, was built. The site was discovered by RAF aerial reconnaissance photography in the exceptionally dry summer of 1929 when two concentric circles 75m diameter were recognised as henges. Excavation revealed pottery shards and other indicators of human activity. The area seems to have had special religious significance, maybe it's mere coincidence but close by and three thousand years later the Romans built a stone temple to their gods at nearby Caister St Edmund.

Left:

ARMINGHALL CAR BOOT SALE

Whoever is in charge of car parking for this weekly event certainly has a flair for organisation!

ATTLEBOROUGH TOWN CENTRE

The original route of the A11 runs through the centre of the town. The parish church sits on an island of one-way traffic. In the churchyard are roses bred by Chelsea Gold Medallist, Peter Beales, whose nursery is on the town's southern edge. The war memorial near the church is unusual in that it commemorates soldiers killed in the Crimean War.

ATTLEBOROUGH
From 1896 until very recently Gaymers Cider Works (the extensive building complex to the right of the railway line) was one of the town's principal employers – currently it's a chicken processing plant. In 1984 the long-overdue bypass was a blessed relief to this small market town.

AUTUMN IN THE BRECKS

Timber worth £4m is harvested annually from the Forestry Commission's trees in Breckland, mostly to be turned into pallets, chipboard and decking. The recently felled areas (brown) will be replanted either with identical species or with a different crop should disease control be necessary. Some Breckland areas have been awarded SSSI status because of their importance as wildlife habitats. The rare red squirrel is one inhabitant of these sandy soils.

Right: **AUTUMN OVERHEAD WHITLINGHAM**

AYLSHAM

The town retains its central market place with a regular weekly market. John O' Gaunt, believed to be the founder of the parish church, is depicted on horseback on the town sign. Excavations for the bypass revealed evidence of Bronze and Iron Age settlements. Norfolk's only railway tunnel in current use runs under the bypass over the track of the Bure Valley Railway. The tunnel didn't exist when the line, originally the East Norfolk Railway, ran a full-size track operation and traversed a remote country lane by means of a level crossing. But level crossings aren't compatible with road traffic travelling at speed so a tunnel was built to accommodate the narrow gauge Bure Valley trains and the quiet lane became the bypass. The line can be traced snaking through the town with the white-painted former crossing keeper's cottage in the foreground.

AYLSHAM: ST MICHAEL'S HOSPITAL

Built in 1849 as a parish workhouse by Swaffham-born architect William Donthorne whose specialisms seem to have been workhouses (Ely, Wisbech, Downham Market) and grand houses (Cromer Hall, Pickenham Hall, Hillington Hall). Donthorne's style might best be described as 'Tudor Gothic'. This rather forbidding-looking building is now in the process of being converted into private houses and apartments having become a hospital when the workhouse closed. The two turrets at the front of the main building house circular staircases. Only the single storey rectangular building (right of picture) is now in use by the NHS.

BARNHAM BROOM

Lying in the Yare Valley west of Norwich this is a fertile area especially suitable for arable farming. The river Yare and the mill are in the foreground. Broom grew abundantly around the river in Tudor times hence the name.

BARTON BROAD

The River Ant flows through this, the second largest of the Norfolk Broads. Limekiln Dyke (centre left) leads to Neatishead where the floating base belonging to the Nancy Oldfield Trust is moored each summer at the dyke entrance. At the top of the broad a short channel to the left leads to Barton Turf whilst the main river is the right-hand channel leading to Wayford Bridge where it becomes the navigation known as the Dilham and North Walsham Canal. The triangular piece of vegetation between the two channels is described on maps as 'The Heater' the origin of which comes from the name and shape of an old fashioned flat iron. In the middle of the broad is what remains of Pleasure Hill, originally a causeway separating the peat digging areas of two parishes, but a century or more ago it had eroded to become a small island and in the Victorian era was a favourite picnic site. Recent extensive replanting round the edge has halted erosion.

BARTON TURF

The hamlet at the top of Barton Broad (no shop no pub) is a mecca for sailing dinghies. In the 19th century the village was commercially busy, as the existing warehouse at the public staithe indicates. A lime kiln stood nearby, chalk was brought in by water and baked to produce lime for both mortar and plaster for the building trade. Lime also was spread on the fields to correct over acidity of the peaty soil. Old records show turves of peat in large quantities were dug from the site of the broad to supply, among others, the monks of Norwich cathedral, hence the name Barton Turf.

BAWDESWELL

Geoffrey Chaucer's Reeve in *The Canterbury Tales* (c.1386) came from Bawdeswell.

> *'Of Northfolk was this reve of which I tell*
> *Bisyde a toun men clepen Baldeswelle'.*

Timber-framed Chaucer House stands in the main street. In November 1944 a Mosquito bomber returning to its base at Downham Market from a raid over Germany encountered severe icing and crashed on to the church killing both crew members. Ten years later the church was rebuilt in American Colonial style causing one parishioner to remark that the building would look more at home in Norfolk, Virginia.

FLORANOVA AT BAWDESWELL

It's impressive on the ground but this display by plant breeders Floranova looks even more spectacular from the air. Is it fanciful to imagine that it portrays a florid face?

BAWSEY RUIN

There was a church here at the time of the Norman Conquest. In Domesday Book 1086 it's listed as part of an agricultural settlement called Bowesia (in translation 'Gadfly Island'). A Neolithic axe handle, a Bronze Age round burial barrow, an Iron Age gold torc, Saxon medieval pottery and gravestones, all have been discovered on this slightly elevated site near present-day Kings Lynn. The Timewatch Team fronted by TV's Tony Robinson found a skeleton whose skull had suffered a blow to the head. And small boys playing by the Gaywood River 70 years ago used to unearth human bones. There's evidence that there was a settlement here until the 16th century when the landowner turfed out the inhabitants in order to extend his farming enterprises, much like the Highland Clearances. The church fell into disrepair but was left standing for fear of the wrath of god on whoever demolished it. There's confusion among the reference books as to whether the church was dedicated to St Mary or St James.

BAYFIELD HALL

Home of 'benevolent squire' Sir Alfred Jodrell who created the model village of Glandford over a century ago. The Elizabethan Bayfield Hall was built by the Jermy family and gentrified with a new front when acquired by the Jodrells. The ruined church of St Margaret's was still in use in 1603 but was derelict by the end of the 18th century.

BEESTON HALL

The ornamental lake becomes a small stream flowing off-picture into Limekiln Dyke and hence into Barton Broad. The gothic-style hall (1786) is faced with square-knapped flint. It was built by Jacob Preston and replaced an earlier hall on the site, both halls have been in the Preston family since their creation. A Thomas Preston was British Consul at Ekaterinburg in central Russia at the time of the Russian Revolution (1917) and was implicated in plans to rescue Czar Nicholas II in 1918. For this Thomas Preston was sentenced to death but the sentence was not carried out. The hall, occasionally open to the public, contains Russian mementoes.

BINHAM PRIORY

The Benedictine order of monks founded their priory here around 1091 and it flourished until the Dissolution (1536–40). Bit by bit the Priory fell into decay and the building materials were recycled into the fabric of some of the older cottages. Fortuitously the nave was left more or less intact and became the parish church, it remains so today. From the extensive ruins it's possible to recognise certain monastic offices but not to imagine the lives of the monks whose days began at 2am with prayers followed by seven more services before bed at 8pm!

BIRCHAM NEWTON

RAF Bircham Newton was created during WW1 and in WW2 was used by Coastal Command and Air Sea Rescue. Since 1966 it has been occupied by the Construction Industry Training Board (CITB).

BLAKENEY CHURCH

The church today is surrounded by relatively few buildings because a fire destroyed the first village houses which were grouped around the church. The people moved down towards the drained marshes and the sea. Fishing was an important local industry. The small tower has the appearance of being tacked on to the north-east corner of the chancel and was equipped with a light which served as a shipping beacon.

Left:

BLICKLING

Blickling Hall (c1620) in all its Jacobean splendour, jewel in the crown of the National Trust's Norfolk properties. The estate, over which there are footpaths, extends to almost 5000 acres. If Anne Boleyn *was* born here, as some historians believe, then it would have been in the former house on the site.

BLOFIELD

This is one of the few Norfolk villages having permanent traffic lights. Until the 1990s the village had a Magistrates' Court (to sentence motorists jumping the lights?). Justice had been meted out here for a long time because before the courtroom was built magistrates sat at the nearby Globe public house. A corn grinding mill stood where Mill Close is now. A tragedy occurred when the sweep of the sails killed a child standing underneath. The sails were subsequently shortened.

BOWTHORPE

Rebel farmer Robert Kett camped here at Bowthorpe with his army of dissidents, mostly tradesmen and small farmers, en route to Norwich to protest both against the enclosure of common land and freedom to work the land. Although Kett became a popular local hero it didn't do him much good because he ended up hanging from the battlements of Norwich Castle.

Bowthorpe is now a suburb of Norwich. The sand and gravel pits through which the River Yare flows were excavated mostly after WW2 for road building. To the right of the pits lies Bowthorpe Nature Reserve.

BRANDISTON

Lying about five miles south-west of Aylsham the oldest building in the picture is the bottom half of the church tower. Norman in origin, the octagonal top was added 200 years later together with the nave and chancel. Brandiston Hall (lying back from the church and mid picture) was built in 1647 and much enlarged in 1875.

BRECKLAND

In 1894 naturalist W G Clarke coined the word 'Breckland'. The 'breck' or break arising from the medieval system of cultivating this poor sandy soil one year in ten, leaving the land fallow for the following nine years, had been practised for centuries. Breckland is defined as being an area of sandy heathland, ponds and meres which lies between the chalk uplands of East Anglia to the north-east and The Fens to the west. The Meres (pools) lie within SSSIs and the whole is designated as being an environmentally sensitive area. The landscape remained unchanged for thousands of years until the planting of thousands of acres of trees by the Forestry Commission began about a hundred years ago. Nevertheless there remain vast areas of Breckland heathland.

BREKLES/BRECCLES/BRECKLES HALL

The moated Elizabethan hall in Breckland was built for the Woodhouse family c1583 with additions in the 19th century by Edwin Lutyens. The hall has a priest's hole as did many other of the grand houses owned by Catholic families at the time of the upset brought about by the Reformation (Oxburgh was another). Pevsner states that the Mrs Woodhouse of 1583 was referred to as 'a popish seducing recusant'. The 19th century author, antiquary and Rector of Scarning, Dr Jessop, said of Breccles that 'It is one of those houses which if not haunted ought to be'.

BROGRAVE MILL (1771)

The mill's stumpy shape is typical of the earlier tower mills. Until 1930 the mill drained the Brograve Level marshes into Waxham New (new in 1820) Cut. The Cut, now only deep enough for canoes and the like, ran for six kilometres from Horsey Mere to the brickworks at Lound Bridge.

BROOME PLACE
The original mellow brick house (1700) situated on the Norfolk/Suffolk border near Bungay underwent considerable alteration by Norfolk architect Basil Cozens-Hardy in 1887.

BURNHAM THORPE PARSONAGE

The house in which Horatio Nelson was born (1758) has been replaced by the one shown. It was from the earlier house that Admiral Nelson for five years tended his father's glebe lands while exiled on half pay before the start of the Revolutionary Wars . The Reverend Edmund Nelson, had the livings and therefore the glebe lands of Burnham Ulph and Burnham Norton in addition to those at Burnham Thorpe.

CAISTER DIG 2009

During the summer of 2009 students from Nottingham University with local input from the Norfolk Archaeology Service excavated Venta Icenorum, established here in the 5th century. It's fortunate that the growing Saxon settlement at Norwich arose around the River Wensum rather than here at Caister near the River Tas, thereby leaving Venta Icenorum more easily accessible for excavation today. The site was discovered during an RAF flight in the very dry summer of 1929.

CAISTER SKELETON

The most exciting recent find has been a skeleton of someone who met a violent end as the dent to his skull indicates.

Right:

CAISTER ROMAN TOWN

Venta Icenorum was the capital of the Iceni tribe but following the Roman victory over the Iceni who were led by Boadicea, Roman ways of life were imposed upon the conquered tribe. The straight lines and grids we associate with Roman planning is evident here at the excavated site. Buildings thought to have been temples, an amphitheatre, the forum (market place) and houses have been evident in a succession of archaeological digs.

CASTLE RISING

The Norman keep, to which treacherous and scheming Queen Isabella, the 'She-Wolf of France' and mother of Edward III, was banished. The castle was built by William de Warenne, henchman of William the Conqueror.

CATTON PARK

This 74-acre parkland two miles outside Norwich originally was part of the 18th century Catton Park estate. The Hall has been divided into apartments and is surrounded by modern houses. The parkland is now a Trust-owned public space. Regeneration began in 2005. BBC 'Springwatch, visited in 2008 and restored the Victorian pond. Footpaths have been created and the whole park made more 'wildlife friendly'.

CAWSTON MANOR

There's been a house on the site for several centuries but the present one was designed by the distinguished Victorian architect Sir Ernest George in 1896 for a George Cawston (presumed a coincidence that Cawston's house was in Cawston village). The Manor has undergone several changes both of use and of ownership. Built as a private residence, in WW1 it was a Military Hospital, in WW2 a Children's Home and more recently a Private School then a Spiritual Healing Centre. The lake was made by damming the picturesquely named Mermaid Stream, a tributary of the River Wensum.

COCKLEY CLEY

The Hall, built in the then fashionable Italianate style, dates from 1870 and looks to be a straightforward solid building. Less straightforward are three mysteries about the surrounding village, the most gruesome being the finding of the headless body of a woman in the 1970s. Although the body was exhumed only a few years ago the mystery of her identity and that of her killer remains unknown. Less macabre is the name of the pub 'Twenty Churchwardens'. Why so many? And what were they doing at the pub? Twenty churchwardens was the sum total of churchwardens in the group of parishes including Cockley Cley. And what about the village's quaint name? Cley is Old English for 'clayey soil' but Cockley? It may mean 'cock wood' or 'a wood frequented by wild birds' or, according to the experts, its origins may be lost... yet another mystery.

COMBINING WHEAT

July and August (and if it's a wet summer, September) sees the harvest under way in the Eastern Counties, the principal grain growing area in the country. Combine harvesters have very sophisticated controls and can cost a small fortune.

CROMER LOOKING WEST
Norfolk's favourite holiday resort.

CROMER: LOOKING AFTER THE ENVIRONMENT

Opposite North Norfolk District Council's headquarters is the new Police Station with a 'green' (sedum) roof. Green roofs are claimed to offer better insulation than roof tiles and to play their part in reducing carbon dioxide emissions. In the foreground are 10 pitches funded by a government 'Gypsy and Traveller' grant. Travellers and gypsies are allowed on to this site for a limited period whilst looking for alternative accommodation.

CREAKE ABBEY
The abbey in the village of North Creake was founded in 1206 by the Augustinian Canons. At the Reformation it went into voluntary liquidation thereby avoiding wholesale destruction. Abbey Farm, built in the grounds, contains stones from the abbey building.

DEREHAM

Properly called East Dereham, to distinguish it from the smaller West Dereham near Downham Market, the town sign omits the East. The A47 with its fast traffic travelling west to the Midlands and east to Norwich and Great Yarmouth now bypasses the town but the more leisurely Mid Norfolk Railway brings all road traffic to a halt as, at snail's pace, it crosses one of the town's main roads.

DERSINGHAM

A bypass divides the village from farming land which was under water during the 1953 floods. The dark-green rectangle in the arable area is the remains of a wildfowl decoy. The village on the skyline (top right) is Snettisham where an important hoard of Iron Age treasure was ploughed up in 1948 and on subsequent occasions, the last find being in 1990. The Snettisham Hoard consisted of gold torcs and other artefacts dating from 100BC. The treasures are today in the British Museum and Norwich Castle Museum.

DIDLINGTON

All that's left of this once magnificent country estate is the complex of pools and a few buildings (the coach house, the clock tower, the stables, some boathouses and a folly). Improvements were made to an existing house, including the addition of an Italianate-style front, in the 1850s. Subsequent owners added to the fabric and filled the house with their extensive collection of ancient Egyptian artefacts. The artefacts have been claimed to have been the inspiration for the chosen career of Egyptologist Howard Carter, credited with having discovered the tomb of Tutankhamun. In WW2 the house was HQ for the planning of the Normandy landings but in 1950 the contents were sold off and the house demolished. More recently buildings on the estate have been converted to private houses and today it's possible to take a tour of what remains.

DISS TOWN CENTRE

Poet John Betjeman voted Diss his favourite town but its popularity today lies not only in its concentration of old buildings and narrow streets but in its fast rail service to London. Unlikely though it may have seemed even 60 years ago Diss today is in easy commuting distance. But on a far less immediate and worldly note the Manning family were rectors of the Parish Church in an unbroken line from 1778 to 1916.

Right:

DISS MERE

The 6-acre mere is almost certainly of the same origin as the nearby Breckland Meres i.e. there's no apparent surface stream supplying water, but there's an underlying chalk seam preventing water flowing away.

In harsh winters the Mere freezes over allowing skating, and in a very hard freeze horses and carts have been recorded driving from one side to the other.

DOCKING WORKHOUSE

The Union Workhouse (a union of several parishes) was built in 1835 at a cost of £9000. Now divided into single units it provides both permanent and holiday homes, each one costing considerably more than that!

EARSHAM HALL

As with the fortunes of many large country houses the hall has undergone several transformations. It's widely believed that some of the early renovations were paid for with money from the slave trade. Until the present owner began a furniture business with a café and functions venue, the building previously housed a private school. Built in the 17th century with 18th and 19th century additions the red brick house with its extensive outbuildings has an air of elegance.

EAST CARLETON: THE GROVE CHESHIRE HOME

The Cheshire Homes were set up by Group Captain Leonard Cheshire (1917–1992) and his wife Sue Ryder to give shelter to people with disabilities. Leonard Cheshire was one of the most highly decorated bomber pilots (VC, OM, DFC, DSO) of WW2. He married Sue Ryder in 1959. Baroness Ryder's charitable work also includes care for the disabled. The Grove was the name of the previous building on the site.

Right:

EAST HARLING

The light, dry, sandy soils of Breckland always have been particularly suitable for sheep grazing. There used to be a lamb market here hence the lamb on the village sign. The church is considered to be one of the most magnificent in the area, the east window second only to that in St Peter Mancroft, Norwich. East Harling played its part in the Napoleonic Wars. On Telegraph Hill, not far from the disused wind-mill, stood a telegraph station, part of the shutter signals chain which connected The Admiralty in London with ships anchored off Great Yarmouth.

EASTMERE

Does this church look somewhat artificial? Possibly resembling a model village? That's because it's a full scale *model* of a church! It's part of the artificial village of Eastmere created within the STANTA area (the Stanford Training Area aka the Battle Area) and used by the military of several nations for training.

In 1942 30 000 acres including four villages were commandeered by the army as a training ground with the understanding that when hostilities were over the villagers would be able to return to their homes. This has never happened. The public are excluded from the whole area except in special situations. Many outside scenes for 'Dad's Army' were filmed in the Battle Area in the 1960s.

EASTMERE TRAINING VILLAGE

Eastmere 'village' was designed to train soldiers for action in Northern Europe and to learn anti-terrorism techniques relevant during the Northern Ireland conflict. The flat roofed buildings resembling Middle Eastern houses have been added more recently. Grenade craters surround the village houses.

Left:

EAST WRETHAM NATURE RESERVE

Ringmere (left foreground), Fenmere (centre) and Langmere (right) are three of the nine Breckland Meres which are fed, uniquely, from underground chalk aquifers and not from surface water. It was here that in the 10th century one of the last and most bloody battles in East Anglia was fought between the indigenous Saxons and invading Danes as recorded in the Anglo Saxon Chronicle – a forerunner of the Eastern Daily Press? The A1075 Watton to Thetford road runs close to Ringmere and is crossed by an ancient Drove Road.

FAKENHAM RACECOURSE

The racecourse was created here in 1905 for National Hunt race meetings. The steeplechase course sits outside the hurdle course and is 1 mile in circumference. Meetings are held from October to May.

FAKENHAM TOWN

FENLAND DRAINAGE – STOWBRIDGE

The bridge crosses the River Great Ouse (left) and the Flood Relief Channel which meet further north to empty into The Wash.
Attempts to drain The Fens had been undertaken in the past, particularly by a group of businessmen called The Merchant Adventurers in the 15th century with wealth created from wool. But when in the 17th century the 4th Duke of Bedford brought over from Holland the drainage expert Cornelius Vermuyden to devise a drainage scheme for the waterlogged marshes, Fenland agriculture changed for ever. Fertile peat soil was made workable and yielded so well that to the present day its sale yields a premium. In some areas the peat is now almost worked out but that's another story.

FRAMINGHAM PIGOT

This church is a Victorian gem. Consecrated in 1859 and costing £4,500 it replaced an earlier one on the same site. The body of the church is faced with square knapped flints. Flint is a local, durable and beautiful building material. The stone tower with its octagonal lantern turret and spire is curious. It stands on the NW corner of the nave in a somewhat 'add on' fashion. There are no stone quarries in Norfolk so the material would have had to have been brought in. The four lucarne windows (small openings to let in light high up in the spire) face in the directions of the cardinal points of the compass. Electric lighting was not installed until the 1950s, two oil lamps remain on the chancel walls as a reminder.

FRETTENHAM

This was the last corn grinding mill (1870) to be built in Norfolk. In 1900 the sails turned for the last time. The forty seven feet high five storeyed mill recently has been restored to provide residential accommodation, the cap is shallower than the original.

GODWICK LOST VILLAGE

Godwick was an impoverished village with a population in decline until the *c*15 when the remaining inhabitants packed up and left for reasons unknown. One speculation is that its heavy wet land made farming difficult. The church tower, whose origins are thought to be Norman, was converted into a folly in the *c*17 but in 1981 part of it collapsed. English Heritage by arrangement with the owner administers the site which is open during the summer months.

GREAT HOCKHAM HALL
The Grade II listed Queen Anne (1702) house is in the heart of Breckland. A new feature is the group of five water-filled trapezoid shapes in front of the house. The containers are replenished by rainwater run off from the Hall roof. Great Hockham village is in the distance.

HAINFORD HALL

Where once horse-driven carriages trundled up to the front door of this rather forbidding looking Georgian house now old bangers come to die – or in modern jargon are recycled. This is a scrapyard where starter motors or dynamos, gear boxes or whole engines can be obtained for a car which rolled off the production line many miles ago. The hall has been unoccupied since 1940 and is now in a poor state of repair but the yard surrounding it has never been busier.

HARDINGHAM HALL
The oldest part of the hall is 18th century with Victorian and Edwardian additions 'all remarkably and tactfully well done' according to Pevsner. Part of a crinkle crankle wall is in the background.

HARDLEY MILL

Hardley Drainage Mill on the banks of the River Yare operated from 1874 until c.1950 when an electric pump took over. As was the fate of so many similar mills it was abandoned to wind and weather but rescued in 1991 when the Hardley Windmill Trust began its restoration. In October 2009 the sails turned again. Once a new turbine pump is installed and the sluice gates are reassembled, the mill pump will resume its original job of pumping water from the surrounding dykes into the river. It's accessible on foot via the Wherryman's Way footpath or from the River Yare where pontoon mooring and electricity hookups have been installed. There's a Visitor Centre.

HELICOPTER RESCUE

An RAF Sea King helicopter in a practice rescue with an inshore lifeboat in attendance.

HETHEL CHURCH

The chancel of All Saints' Church was extended northwards early in the 18th century to provide a mausoleum for the Branthwaite family. Visually it's an uncomfortable addition. The base of the tower is thought to be Saxon in origin and so is about the same age as the Hethel Thorn. Alongside a footpath from the churchyard the hawthorn stands in what is the smallest (0.025 hectares) Wildlife Trust Nature Reserve in the country.

Right: **HICKLING BROAD AND BEYOND**

The proximity of the coast demonstrates The Broads' vulnerability to flooding. In 1953 the breach at Horsey Mere (centre right) covered thousands of acres of marsh and arable land with salt water. Livestock drowned and the damage took years to overcome. Hickling has the largest expanse of open water of all the Broads (six hundred hectares approx.). The navigation channel is only 1.5m deep.

The Norfolk Wildlife Trust manages the whole; the marsh is grazed by horses and the reed beds are cut for thatching, only the birds and mammals are in their natural habitats and even they are protected by man and by legislation.

In the picture Hickling Broad is to the left and below it Heigham Sound and Duck Broad leading out on to the River Thurne. To the right is Horsey Mere which is joined to Heigham Sound by Meadow Dyke. Foreground right is the River Thurne and the shallow Martham Broad. A navigation channel runs across the broad and ends at Somerton Staithe.

HILBOROUGH HOUSE

This imposing house of brick and flint in Queen Anne style was built as recently as 1996-9. The formal gardens continue the Dutch influence and were designed by Chelsea Gold Medallist Arne Maynard whose special skill is to create a garden which blends perfectly with the house it surrounds.

HOME PLACE AT HIGH KELLING

Home Place originally was called 'Voewood', then later Kelling Place and recently it has reverted to the original. The house is considered to be one of the very best examples of the 'Arts and Crafts' movement. The movement harked back to the Renaissance with its concentration on local materials and traditional styles.

Built by Edward Prior 1903-5 for a wealthy clergyman, the house cost the astonishingly high sum of £60 000. Its 'butterfly' plan was a device used to take advantage of attractive views and of sunlight from as many rooms as possible. Built of local flint over local carstone with Norfolk roof pantiles nonetheless the construction included modern technology in the use of reinforced concrete. The house's early years were not happy. Shortly after its completion a sanatorium was built next door and Voewood's mistress, fearing she would contract tuberculosis, decided she could no longer live in the house. For many years it was rented out or was in institutional use but in more recent years it has returned to private ownership.

HUNSTANTON – Wreck of the *Sheraton*

Built in 1907 as a fishing vessel, in WW1 the thirty-nine metre boat was involved in boom defence work and in WW2 was a patrol vessel. Wrecked in 1947 she was moored in The Wash for target practice but broke loose and drifted on to Hunstanton beach near the lighthouse. Her ferrous metal was sold for salvage but even today a section of hull lies uncovered on the beach at various states of the tide.

IRRIGATION ON THE RAVENINGHAM ESTATE

The five-acre lake was created as a millennium project. Its clay liner was made by soil excavations for the two irrigation reservoirs on the farm and holds a total of thirty-five million gallons. Raveningham Hall (18th century with later additions) absorbed the round-towered church into its grounds as did so many country estates. The church's exterior has been cemented over, probably for practical reasons, but visually it disappoints.

IRRIGATION ON A GRAND SCALE
Here at Acle the extra-wide sprayer booms water this potato field with minimum disturbance to the crop.

KETTERINGHAM HALL AND CHURCH

The hall, with church in close proximity, nicely encapsulate the power-struggle between the 19th century squire Sir John Boileau and the vicar the Reverend William Wayte Andrew. The struggle is documented in Owen Chadwick's book *Victorian Miniature*. Fortunately for the vicar the living was not in the gift of the squire, moreover the vicar had substantial private means which gave him a greater degree of independence than many of his contemporary clergy. There was no house with the living so the Reverend Andrew and his family made their home at Wood Hall, Hethersett, a couple of miles away. For over thirty years from the Vicar's arrival at Ketteringham in 1835 until the squire's departure in 1868 the squire and parson performed what they considered to be their duties regardless of the other and with much acrimony on both sides.

From 1942-45 Ketteringham Hall was the HQ of the 2nd US Air Division of the 8th USAAF in Norfolk. In the grounds there's a memorial plaque to those who had served. The hall has now been converted into offices.

KIMBERLEY HALL

The house was begun in 1712, added to in 1759 and has since been remodelled several times, including following the WW2 occupation by the Army. It had been in the hands of the Wodehouse family (of which Jeeves' creator P G Wodehouse was a distant member) in an unbroken line until its sale in 1958.

KINGS LYNN: PALM PAPER

The £400 million paper and pulp mill on the site of the former sugar beet processing factory has brought one-hundred-and-fifty new jobs into the area. The factory takes its water from the relief channel of the River Ouse. Named after its Chief Executive Dr Wolfgang Palm, the plant recycles newspapers and magazines to provide yet more newsprint along with corrugated cardboard. Five-hundred tonnes of used paper are returned to the plant each week. Archant was Palm Paper's first customer so the paper on which the EDP is printed may have made several trips to the plant already. Talk about old news! 500,000 tonnes of used paper produces 400,000 tonnes of new material. The round building (bottom right) is a salt barn for Norfolk County Council's Highways Department.

LANDFILL ANCIENT-AND-MODERN AT ALDEBY

In an attempt to harvest resources, trials have been carried out to harness the methane gas given off by decomposition. The pit has been lined to prevent leaching and pipes installed for gas collection. Currently there are one-hundred-and-seventy-four UK landfill projects ongoing as part of the Non Fossil Fuel Obligation.

Right:

LANGHAM

The airfield played a vital role in WW2. Opened in 1940 with grass runways its first function was as an emergency landing ground as a satellite of RAF Bircham Newton Coastal Command. Concrete runways were added during the course of the war. The concrete runways are now used as bases for turkey-rearing sheds – the turkeys never take off except en route to the slaughterhouse. Although the RAF airfield closed down in 1959, aviation continues there. A light-aircraft engineer operating off a grass strip carries on a business maintaining vintage aircraft and it's a familiar site to see a Tiger Moth or Rapide aircraft flying over the saltmarshes much as in a 1930s poster! Part of the airfield was used in 'The Dambusters' film.

LANGLEY ABBEY

What a damp, cold, miserable site on the marshes, less than a mile from the River Yare, this place must have been when the sixteen or so White Canons built their Abbey here in 1195. Nor would white habits seem to have been the most practical garments on such a muddy site. The Canons belonged to the Premonstratensian Order (from their foundation in Prémontré, France). They followed the gentle teaching of St Augustine but not always to the letter it would seem. In 1491, in an argument, a Canon cut off the hand of a Friar. Nor were they much good at trading, a Tuesday Market was granted to the Abbey in 1198 but the monks abandoned it in 1343 because their income was reduced by flooding and 'by excessive hospitality'.

After the Dissolution (1536) most of the buildings fell into disrepair but the cellarium (the west range of the cloister) remains in use as a barn where, in a recent initiative, the early story of Langley Abbey is told. Well-presented information boards, enhanced lighting and access to parts of the building which would have been in use in the 12th century all give some idea of what the Abbey would have been like. The addition of an excellent teashop cum restaurant has made this a well-appointed visitor attraction. The present farmhouse was built in the 18th century.

Left: **LANGHAM VILLAGE**

A distinguished village inhabitant was Captain Frederick Marryat who gave up a career at sea to write books and be a farmer. He was better at the former than the latter although he knew a thing about man-management and appointed the local poacher as his gamekeeper. His best known books are *Mr Midshipman Easy, Masterman Ready* and *Children of the New Forest*. He's buried in the churchyard.

LANGLEY HALL aka LANGLEY PARK now LANGLEY SCHOOL

Sometimes described as 'one of the little known grand houses of Norfolk' (along with Kimberley and Wolterton) the red-brick house was designed by Norwich's Matthew Brettingham who had a hand in the building of Holkham Hall. Langley's Greek Doric porch came later, as did Sir John Soane's pair of elegant lodges, now looking somewhat sorry standing at the former hall entrance on the A146 Norwich Road.

THE LAST SURVIVING STEAM-POWERED HERRING DRIFTER

The *Lydia Eva*, built 1930, worked out of Great Yarmouth until 1942 when she was requisitioned by the Royal Navy. In 1972 she was 'rescued' by the Mincarlo Trust and has returned to her home port of Great Yarmouth.

LONG STRATTON: SOUTH NORFOLK DISTRICT COUNCIL OFFICES

This exciting building was designed in 1978 by architect Michael Innes. The building consists of two hexagons with a short tower off to one side. The whole is an ingenious solution to the insertion of a modern functional building into a setting of old houses.

MERTON HALL

The original Hall (c.1620) burned down in 1956 and all that remains is part of the 19th century rebuilding. One of the treasures remaining was a trunk bearing the letters HR and a king's crown. It's believed that since the hall was only a short distance from the Walsingham Way, the trunk may have belonged to Henry VIII who lodged here on a pilgrimage to Walsingham.

MICKLE MERE

Micklemere, Hill Mere (with island) and Rush Mere (the smallest) are three of the nine Breckland Meres. Meres are pools peculiar to Breckland, replenished from chalk strata deep in the soil rather than from an external source or directly from rainfall. Mickle Mere north of the village of Wretham, in around 1868 had a duck decoy on its thirty acres. The Peddars Way runs nearby.

Left:

METHWOLD

Standing on the edge of The Fens, St George's is one of the very few west Norfolk churches with a spire or steeple. And what a spire it is! It rises from the octagonal top stage of the tower, is crocketed (has decoration in the form of leaf shapes at regular intervals along its outside surface), and soars to one-hundred-and-twenty feet. The churchyard, devoid of gravestones, acts as the perfect foil. The spire must have been a welcome landmark in WW2 for crews returning to RAF Methwold and nearby RAF Feltwell.

MILEHAM CASTLE

Immediately after the Norman Conquest, motte (mound) and bailey (enclosure) castles such as this one here at Mileham and at New Buckenham for example were built as a cheap and effective defences. Mileham Castle probably had fallen out of use by 1300. The mound would have been built from the earth taken to make the ditch. Fragments of a former stone keep (the innermost stronghold) have been found on the site.

NORFOLK AND NORWICH HOSPITAL STAFF CAR PARK

With an excess of nine-hundred beds and many Outpatients' Departments, the Norfolk and Norwich Hospital's numerous staff need a large parking area. Was it deliberate that from the air such an interesting pattern of parked cars would emerge?

NORFOLK AND NORWICH UNIVERSITY HOSPITAL

The hospital was opened in 2001. The green-roofed building comprising two semicircles (representing the letter c twice) is the Big C Centre. Patients with cancer can drop in there with friends or family for advice, reassurance and refreshment. Big C is the local Cancer Charity. Profits from our previous 'From The Air' books have been donated to Big C and to other local charities such as the Air Ambulance Service and to EACH (East Anglian Children's Hospices).

Clearly Mike must have taken this picture very early one morning because by 10am on most days it's impossible to find a parking space!

NORFOLK WOODLAND

NORTON'S BROAD aka COCKLE BROAD

This landlocked broad upriver of Wroxham on the River Bure is currently under restoration. The Broads' Authority is working on those sixty-four broads which are considered to have the greatest recovery potential. Upriver broads, cut off from the main rivers, have the greatest chance of retaining freshwater habitats despite anticipated climate change. Norton's Broad together with Belaugh Broad on the Bure's opposite bank is being mud pumped to remove nutrients and create depth. The plan is to have guided canoe trails with access permission from private landowners.

NORWICH: THE GREAT HOSPITAL

Founded in 1249 aged priests, poor scholars, the sick and paupers were cared for at St Helen's in Bishopgate. The chancel ceiling was decorated with two-hundred-and-fifty-two paintings of spreadeagles in commemoration of the visit of Anne of Bohemia in 1383. In the 16th century the nave and chancel were partitioned off at either end to provide ward accommodation for needy men and women. The main body and tower remains to this day as the parish church of St Helen's. At certain times it's possible to visit Eagle Ward where until fairly recently elderly ladies were accommodated in partitioned cubicles, above them the daunting spreadeagle ceiling.

Left:
NORWICH CITY CENTRE

The River Wensum, the Cathedral, the Castle Mound all have great historical importance but so does just about every street and building within this fine city.

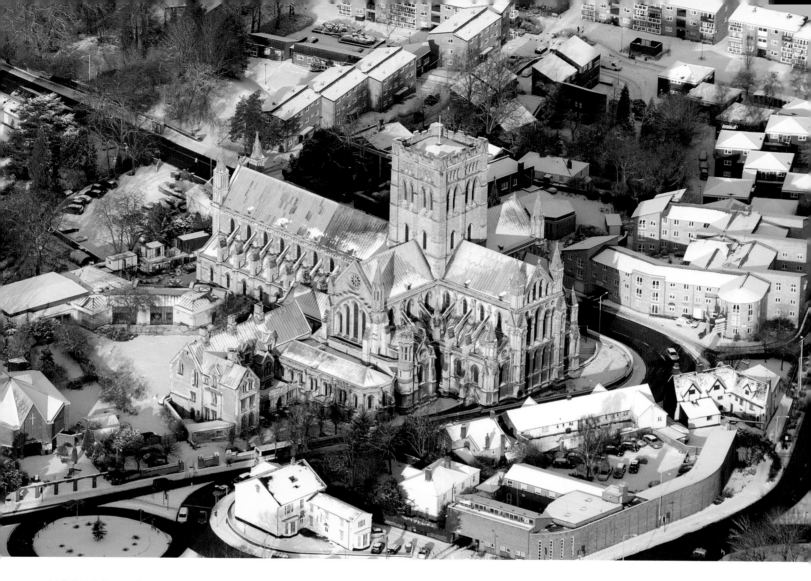

NORWICH ROMAN CATHOLIC CATHEDRAL

Standing on one of the highest points of the city and built on the site of the old city gaol St John's church gained cathedral status in 1976. Work began in 1882 on what was to be the Catholic parish church. The church was a gift to the city from the Duke of Norfolk. The architect Giles Gilbert Scott was awarded the commission. His best known works are perhaps Liverpool's Anglican cathedral (begun 1903) and the red telephone box (1924). He was a convert to Catholicism. During the work on St John's his health deteriorated and his brother John Oldrid Scott took over.

During the annual National Heritage Weekend the church tower is open to the public; the magnificent views over the city justify the climb.

PUDDING NORTON DESERTED VILLAGE

All that remains of the church is this ruined tower described as 'like a broken tooth'. By 1600 the village was deserted and it's probable that landowners had enclosed the land to graze sheep thereby depriving tenants of a living. Pudding Norton Hall survives as do earthworks of former streets and dwellings nearby.

RAF FELTWELL

The radomes (radar domes) were installed by the American National Security Agency some years ago after the RAF vacated the airfield in 1966. Built in 1938 RAF Feltwell originally was a bomber base and had superseded a WW1 base on the south side of the airfield.

RAF NEATISHEAD

The radar station near Horning was once the Radar (Radio Detection and Ranging) Control and Reporting Centre for the whole of the south of England but now it has been downgraded to an RRH station (Remote Radar Head station). It was set up in 1941 to provide radar, ground-to-air radio and data links coverage as part of the UK Surveillance System.

The Radar Museum housed in the original operations building documents the importance of RAF Neatishead from its creation until 1993. The museum traces the history and development of Air Defence Radar since 1935. With the end of the Cold War, secrets such as these could be revealed.

RAF THETFORD aka RAF BARNHAM

An aircraft would have difficulty landing on this tree-strewn area today but during WW1 it was a Royal Flying Corps base. And in 1932 Sir Alan Cobham's Flying Circus arrived. A civic welcome awaited them and the idea of Thetford having a civil airfield was mooted but nothing ever became of the idea. The former airfield was news again in 1953 when an atomic weapons store was installed there (the buildings in the foreground). By 1968 the weapons were obsolete and the site was sold and is now used by light industry.

RAF WEST RAYNHAM

RAF West Raynham, originally a grass airfield, was active from 1939 until 1991. During WW2 it began as a Bomber Command Station operating Blenheim aircraft. Subsequently many aircraft types including Ansons, Gloster Gladiators, the Boeing Flying Fortress, Beaufighters, Mosquitoes and Spitfires were based here. In 1947 the early jet fighters (Vampires and Meteors) were evaluated at the airfield. The 1960s saw interesting action. In March 1967 Hunter aircraft from RAF West Raynham dropped napalm bombs on the wreck of oil tanker 'Torrey Canyon' aground on rocks off the Cornish Coast to try to burn off the spilled crude oil. The oil spillage was one of the worst ever environmental disasters. And in April 1968 a Hunter aircraft broke formation whilst flying back to West Raynham from RAF Tangmere, flew along the Thames and under the top span of Tower Bridge. There's no record of the fate of the Flight Lieutenant at the controls! The station stood empty for some years but recently there have been plans to create an eco-village using the RAF housing. The runways and perimeter tracks are now being broken up to provide crushed concrete for road building.

RAINTHORPE HALL

The original parts of the hall are almost certainly Tudor (c.1503). This view is of the back of the house; note the distinctive polygonal stair turret. The grounds run down to the River Tas a 16th-century fish stewpond – now ornamental – kept the house in valuable protein. A medieval nuttery and knot garden are early garden features. Some of the scenes from the TV production of 'Vanity Fair' were shot here.

REYMERSTON HALL

A nice enough Georgian Hall but the special features are the grass runways for this is the home of Wing Commander Ken Wallis MBE who at a ripe old age continues to fly his gyrocopters – a far cry from the bombers he flew during WW2. His gyrocopter 'Little Nellie' with him at the controls featured in the James Bond film 'You Only Live Twice'.

ROUGHTON

In 1931 this quiet village, three miles from Cromer, gave sanctuary to Nobel Prizewinner Albert Einstein who was fleeing Jewish persecution in Nazi Germany. For several months he lived a low-profile existence in a wooden hut on Roughton Heath (far distance). The modest living quarters were the property of a landowner MP who was assisting in Einstein's escape to America. At Roughton the brilliant scientist had a small band of helpers and a handful of villagers 'in the know' who looked after him. At the entrance to the New Inn on the main road at Roughton there's a plaque commemorating this remarkable wartime concealment.

THE ROYAL NORFOLK SHOW

For two days at the end of June each year the Royal Norfolk Show attracts thousands of visitors. It's the largest agricultural show in the country. There are prizes for the best beef cattle, the most diligent dogs, the smartest sheep, the pertest pigs, the finest flowers, the cutest cockerels, the handsomest hens, and the most gorgeous goats not to mention breeds the forebears of whom would have accompanied Noah into his Ark. The Grand Ring stages events all day, there are trade shows and information tents on all country-related subjects, and a good day out is had by all.

SAHAM TONEY

A Roman settlement existed here. Enamelled pony-harness fittings for a Roman aristocracy were found by 20th-century flint quarriers. Saham Mere, much like Scoulton Mere, lies on the very edge of Breckland. Meres (ponds fed by an underground source rather than from surface water) are a distinctive feature of Breckland. The settlement was listed in the Domesday Book. Saham means 'the lake by the meadow', the manor was held by Roger de Toni in 1199.

SAILING ON THE OUSE
It's hard to imagine that this picture was taken adjacent to King's Lynn Power Station!

SANDRINGHAM

Her Majesty's back garden. The name Sandringham is conjured from the description 'sandy Dersingham'.

SANDRINGHAM PARK HOUSE

The former childhood home of Princess Diana was offered by the Queen to Group Captain Leonard Cheshire in 1983 to convert into a hotel for the disabled and their families.

Right:

THE SANDRINGHAM ESTATE

The 2000-acre estate was bought by Queen Victoria for the Prince of Wales in 1861. On land extending to the tidal mudflats of The Wash, a regime of mixed farming is practised.

During WW1 royal servants, led by King George V's Land Agent, Captain Frank Bett, were recruited from the estate to join the Norfolk Regiment. The Company's annihilation at Gallipoli was told in the TV drama 'All the King's Men' starring David Jason as Frank Bett.

SANTON DOWNHAM

In the 17th century the small village of Santon Downham was almost buried in a sandstorm which lasted for a week and silted up the River Little Ouse. Over centuries sandstorms and windblow have been an ongoing problem in the light Breckland soils but since its foundation in 1919 the Forestry Commission has managed to turn around this formerly unproductive area into a major supplier of softwoods for the building industry.

The Forestry Commission's Eastern Area's HQ is at Santon Downham in what is now Thetford Forest Park where the emphasis is on leisure and conservation.

SCOLT HEAD WRECK

The steam ship *Vina* (built 1894) ended her life ignominiously here off Brancaster as target practice for aircraft preparing for the Normandy landings. Although very little is known of her commercial life it's assumed she was a coastal vessel and carried cargo in her two holds. In 1940 she was used as a naval vessel at Great Yarmouth with plans to fill her with explosives, moor her at the entrance to Yarmouth harbour and cause deliberate chaos by blowing her up in the event of invasion. In 1943 she was towed to her present site and there she remains despite efforts to remove her by various means. But this isn't an entirely negative tale – to local craft she serves as a reminder of the navigational hazards of the sandbank and at least one local family has a beautiful mahogany wardrobe and cupboards with splendid brass fittings all salvaged from the captain's cabin.

SCOLT HEAD

The sandbanks on the island always are on the move but the wreck of the *Vina* (the three black dots in the foreground water) serve as a homing marker from out at sea whatever the state of the tide.

SCULTHORPE

Built in 1942 and during the course of WW2 the airfield was a sometime home base to Free French airmen, squadrons from the Royal New Zealand Air Force, Bomber Command and the USAAF. In the 1950s the airfield was the largest USAAF base in the UK. In the 1970s it was a NATO base until the ending of the Cold War. The impressively long runways have remained unused since the airfield closed in 1992.

SHADWELL PARK

This house is extraordinary. There's intentionally very little symmetry on the outside with an eccentric stair turret attached to the two storeyed entrance tower. The house was built for Sir Robert Buxton c1720. Perhaps it was the original stable block which endeared it to Sheikh Hamdan bin Rashid Al Maktoum, Ruler of Dubai. The Sheikh purchased the estate over 25 years ago to create a thoroughbred racing stud.

SHERINGHAM: A SPECIAL DAY

March 2010 saw the connection of the North Norfolk Railway (The Poppy Line) with the National Rail Network after a gap of forty six years. Britannia Class locomotive 'Oliver Cromwell' traversed the level crossing from the main line on to the Poppy Line track. The Poppy Line runs from Sheringham to Holt on what originally was part of the M&GN (affectionately nicknamed the Muddle & Get Nowhere) track opened in 1887, closed by Dr Beeching 1964, re-opened in stages from 1976.

SHERINGHAM SHOAL WINDFARM

The *Svanen*, a twin-hulled heavy lift floating crane, 100 metres tall, was brought to Sheringham Shoal to install the 90 foundations for the 317MW offshore windfarm. Each foundation weighs around 500 tonnes and is driven up to 36 metres into the seabed. When complete in 2012 the windfarm is expected to generate 1.1TWh per annum or enough electricity to power over 220 000 homes.

SHOTESHAM PARK

The neo-classical building was created by Sir John Soane (c.1785) for Robert Fellowes. Soane's best known works are the Bank of England and his own London house, now a museum, in Lincoln's Inn Fields. Soane was a prolific architect executing commissions all over the country; in Norfolk he designed alterations to Honing Hall. Robert Fellowes's grandfather had bought the Shotesham estate c.1710 and assumed the rôle of country squire. One of the old gentleman's quirks was that he wouldn't allow the congregation (his tenants) into church until he arrived. He then led them in line up the aisle. At the end of the service he's said to have commanded the village constable to be on duty to prevent loitering in the churchyard.

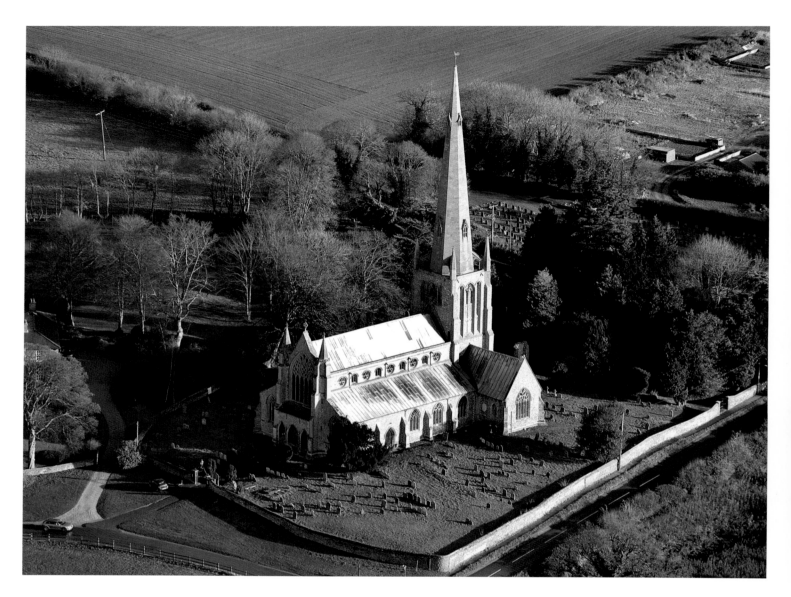

SNETTISHAM CHURCH

St Mary's is one of the very few medieval Norfolk churches with a spire (175 feet). The Cathedral of Fredricton in Canada's New Brunswick Province is said to have been modelled on Snettisham which is somewhat strange as the Norfolk church has a chancel but no nave (demolished). The Canadian copy appears to be minus a nave too.

SOUTH NORFOLK RAPE FIELDS

For about three weeks in June some arable fields are ablaze with bright-yellow oilseed rape flowers. Hay fever sufferers aren't too happy but oilseed rape is a most useful plant which provides vegetable oil for cooking, animal feed and motor fuel.

SOUTH CREAKE – BLOODGATE HILL FORT

The very name Bloodgate sends shivers down the spine and it was here that Saxons fought one of their many battles against Danish invaders. 19th century ploughing has almost levelled this Iron Age single rampart and ditch defence.

SOUTH PICKENHAM HALL

There has been a house on this site since the 17th century, the previous one (1829) having been designed by Donthorne, architect of Aylsham workhouse. Donthorne's house was replaced less than a hundred years later (1903) by this one designed by Weir Schultz a contemporary and acquaintance of some of the most notable of the 'Arts and Crafts' architects. The house is built of Suffolk-made red brick with Ancaster stone used for the main entrance doorway.

SUTTON BRIDGE

Traffic on the A17 between Norfolk and Lincolnshire crosses the River Nene here at Sutton Bridge aka Cross Keys Bridge. The county boundary is a mile to the east but the bridge makes such a cracking picture that Mike justifiably strayed into Lincolnshire air space to capture it. This is the third successive bridge (1897) across the Nene at this point and until the Beeching cuts of 1965 it was used both by rail and road traffic. Shipping entering the river from The Wash require the bridge to swing open to enable craft to reach the port of Wisbech upriver. Had a bridge been here in the 13th century then King John wouldn't have lost his jewels on the causeway running along the edge of the tidal Wash….. or was that tale just a fabrication among the thieving elements in his entourage?

TACOLNESTON (pronounced Tackleston)

The taller 206m (676 feet) mast is in place in preparation for the digital switch over in June 2011. The shorter mast at 165m (541 feet) has until now been the transmitting station for analogue and digital VHF/FM radio and UHF TV transmissions. The first 1994 mast which brought TV to South Norfolk was a mere 61m (200 feet) tall.

Below:

TERRINGTON ST CLEMENT

No one could mistake the combination of flat terrain, a large area of glass houses and the magnificent church for anywhere except Fenland.

THETFORD ALLOTMENTS

Is the allotment an essentially British thing? Certainly all towns and many villages have land rented out for modest sums by local councils enabling self sufficiency in vegetables, flowers too. And often the allotments are sited on marginal land such as here at Thetford, sandwiched between the railway station and the busy road to Swaffham. Inevitably that other British institution, the garden shed, becomes a near essential allotment component – a place in which to store tools and a place in which to shelter from the rain and to store a chair in which to snatch a rest or have a mardle with fellow allotmentees. It's the very sense of order and control which makes the allotment such a fascinating place to see, especially from the air. Straight lines and the textures and colours of different crops turn the picture into a tapestry. What a lot of hard work, expertise and enthusiasm goes into creating that tapestry!

THETFORD MILL

Built to grind corn in the 18th century this mill on the River Thet was known latterly as the 'Coffee Mill'. The stones were by then powered by a turbine to grind the coffee.

There was also a paper mill in the town from which the 18th century historian Francis Blomfield bought his supplies much as the diarist Parson Woodforde did from the paper mill at Swanton Morley.

THOMPSON WATER

Unlike the nine or so meres in Breckland the forty-seven acre Thompson Water is *not* a mere but rather a lake created around 1850 by damming the River Wissey. The Peddars Way runs close by and it's probable that this was a watering place for driven cattle and horses. Thompson Water is now in the care of the Norfolk Wildlife Trust.

THURNE MILL aka MORSE'S MILL
Not every mill is named after someone (usually an owner) but here at Thurne it serves as a memorial to Robert Morse who began the rescue of the derelict mill in 1949. Built in 1820, a third storey was added later giving the whole an untypical look. It had ceased working by 1936.

TIBENHAM

There's been an airfield at Tibenham since WW1. The old airfield was about a mile west of the present one and was a WW1 Class Three Military Landing Ground covering only 30 acres. Defence duties included Zeppelin Patrols using Avro 504s, BE2s, Sopwith Pups and Bristol F2b fighter aircraft. In 1941 the present airfield with concrete runways was made. The US 8th Air Force was assigned here between 1943 nd 1945 operating B24 Liberator Bombers. Lieut. Col. James Stewart (DFC and Croix de Guerre) was wartime Commander of the 703rd Bombardment Squadron. When the Americans left, the airfield was taken over by the RAF to ferry troops home from Italy. In 1959 Tibenham was closed down as a military airfield and became the base for the Norfolk Gliding Club which operates there still.

TILNEY CUM ISLINGTON
Nowhere is Fenland drainage better illustrated then here where most of the houses have desirable water-fronts. The channels join the River Great Ouse further north. Incidentally, the Bailiff's daughter mentioned in the 18th century ballad came from this Islington and not the London one. For those unfamiliar with the story it all ends happily when the knight wins the fair lady (the Bailiff's daughter) after the usual trials and tribulations.

Right:

TRAFFIC JAM
At the junction of the Norwich southern bypass and the A140 Ipswich road eastbound traffic is building and westbound traffic is being allowed through very slowly because of an accident along this always busy road. The Park and Ride car park is to the right. Norwich has more 'Park and Ride' sites (six) than any other city in the country.

TRUCKERS' CONVOY

Annually for the past twenty-four years the East Coast Truckers' Convoy has taken disadvantaged children for a day out at the seaside. Here they are at County Hall assembling for the police escort to Pleasurewood Hills Theme Park at Corton near Lowestoft. Crowds line the whole route to cheer them on their way.

UPTON BROAD AND UPTON LITTLE BROAD

The two broads were originally one and today are cut off from the River Bure. The silted up access channel can be traced as a hedge line some of which now describes a 'V'. The distinctive rectangles to the right of the two broads are Upton Doles, a dole being a portion of grazing land 'doled out' to users and treated as common land except for grazing rights. The straight lines are marshland dykes. Considerable fen restoration around the Broad has been undertaken in recent years by the Norfolk Wildlife Trust. In the middle distance are the two halves of South Walsham Broad, with Malthouse and Ranworth Broads in the far distance. The Fleet Dyke links South Walsham Broad with the River Bure. Halfway along the dyke can be seen the original course of the river around Ward Marsh forming a 'U' with the existing access. On the opposite riverbank lies the mouth of the River Ant and the site of St Benet's Abbey.

WALPOLE ST PETER

This 15th century church is considered to be one of the most beautiful in England. The screen bears a painting of the little known Saint Gudula. A hudd (a portable sentry box) for sheltering the parson at winter funerals stands at the west end of the church, useful before the invention of the umbrella and thermal underwear.

WATTON

The first aircraft to arrive at RAF Watton, once the probability of war became apparent in 1939, was a squadron of Blenheims flying in formation from Eastchurch (Isle of Sheppey). In 1943 the first American units arrived, their job being to salvage and repair B-24 Liberators. In 1944 the Liberators were used to drop agents into Europe. The airfield was handed back to the RAF in 1945, then used by the Army for a while until the land was sold for housing in 1995.

WELLS HARBOUR: THE NEW BASIN

The new harbour is built exclusively for vessels working on the windfarms in the North Sea. First to benefit will be the eighty-eight turbines on Sheringham Shoal in 2011. The new harbour, which runs parallel to the channel to Wells Quay will have a jetty, mooring pontoons and mains services. Its entrance is close to the lifeboat shed. Much dredging has been required and some of the spoil has been used to enclose the new harbour with banks of sand which blend well into the landscape. There will be no public access.

WELLS: LOOKING SEAWARD

WELNEY OUSE WASHES
When the Old Bedford River and the River Delph on the Welney side (village top of picture) and the New Bedford River, aka the Hundred Foot Drain, on the opposite bank are in flood, the A1101 Littleport to Wisbech road becomes impassable necessitating a detour of twenty miles!

WEST ACRE

The order of Black Canons, so called because of their black garb, were priests who followed the example of the communal life of the Apostles and of St Augustine. There were around twenty communities in Norfolk including those at Creake Abbey and Walsingham. At the Dissolution (1536) the Prior received a pension of £40 per annum.

The largest remaining part on the site is a fragment of the gatehouse next to the church and minimal remains of the chapter house and the refectory. Across the River Nar are fragments of the stables. The Priory was on the same impressive scale as Castle Acre Priory two miles to the east.

WHERRY *ALBION*

Albion, then called *Plane*, was rescued in 1949 by a group of people who had the foresight to realise that it was important to preserve for posterity an example of the traditional trading wherry. The wherries worked solely on the Norfolk Broads and rivers with a small amount of lightering work in harbours. Built for Walkers, Maltsters of Bungay, *Albion* is unique in having a carvel (smooth) hull best suited for the lock chambers of the Bungay Navigation. Albion has recently undergone a major restoration and each winter volunteers work on the wherry to keep her sailing. It says much for the skill of the wherryman that it was reckoned on approaching a bridge the mast could be lowered, the boat pass under the bridge and the mast raised again all whilst under way!

WHERRY *ALBION* AT HUNSETT MILL

The drainage mill and the marshman's cottage were built on the banks of the River Ant in 1860. The mill worked for forty years before being replaced by a mechanical pump. A recent and clever restoration and enlargement of the cottage ensures that from the river there's very little visual intrusion. The extension 'retreats' from the river and most of the new building opens up away from it. Innovations have ensured that the house is almost self sufficient in resources. Solar panels, ground source heat pumps, water from the well and an individual sewage treatment plant together make very few demands on conventional energy supplies.

WICKLEWOOD

This former workhouse (1776) euphemistically called a 'house of industry' is one of the earliest in the county. Its building predated the Poor Law Amendment Act of 1834 which ruled for much harsher treatment of the unfortunate inmates; after the 1834 Act married couples were separated from each other as were children from their parents. Now converted into flats and houses we went to investigate the low structure in the middle of the front lawn. It turned out to be merely an ornamental space with a roof. But driving round to the back of the huge building we came upon an area set apart and marked with a cross. It turned out to be a poignant memorial to the paupers buried within the grounds but was dated as recently as 1926 i.e. within living memory! How times have changed thank goodness.

WIGGENHALL ST GERMANS

The original pump was built in 1934 to take water from the Middle Level Drain into the tidal Great Ouse. The new pump has a 40 per cent increased capacity and should give flood protection to 20 000 homes and to agricultural land. The picture shows the temporary coffer dam (building nearest the river) which excluded water enabling work on the new pumping station (inside the coffer dam) to continue uninterrupted.

The old pumping station (foreground) is being demolished.

WIGGENHALL ST PETER

Pevsner described this derelict church as 'an excellent ruin because the walls stand all the way up and only the roofs are gone'. The ruin lies below the level of the banks of the River Great Ouse.

Within Fenland there are two Terringtons, three Tilneys, two Walpoles and four Wiggenhalls. With the exception of Tilney cum Islington the villages additionally assume the name of the saint to whom their church is dedicated.

WINDFARM
Where's the wind?

WISSINGTON

Here on the banks of the River Wissey lies British Sugar's largest refinery. Built in 1925, coal-fired and served initially by rail and river, the plant is now entirely dependent on the road system. As a contribution to the government's commitment to produce a cleaner road fuel the plant produces bioethanol from vegetable waste in the form of any beet surplus to requirements. Experimentation here is ongoing to produce an even more advanced fuel – biobutanol.

WROXHAM/HOVETON

Although most often referred to as Wroxham this is the village of Hoveton. When over a hundred years ago Roys claimed to be the 'The Largest Village Store in the World' they claimed also to be in Wroxham, presumably because 'Roys of Hoveton' didn't have the same alliterative ring. And they've traded as 'Roys of Wroxham' ever since.

ROYS FIRE 1995
Wherever there's action there's Mike with his camera!

WROXHAM BRIDGE
The Gateway to The Broads across the River Bure from Wroxham (left) to Hoveton (right).

WYMONDHAM TOWN CENTRE

The market held here every Friday was introduced by the monks of Wymondham Priory around 1100. The Great Fire of Wymondham (1615) destroyed most of the buildings in the town centre including the original market cross.

HIGH LEVEL OVER WYMONDHAM

Mercifully the busy A11 now bypasses this small market town and is the third successive road designated A11. The first ran right through the middle of town (showing as a thin straight line centre picture), the second skirted the town edge until the edge was eroded by new houses (the curved line centre picture). The latest A11 (left of picture) is fast and dualled and that should be sufficient for the moment. Or should it? Several thousand new houses are planned for Wymondham and many of the residents are none too happy about it. The sandy area (foreground) is... you've guessed it... the start of a new housing estate.

The heading for the following pictures correctly would read GREAT Yarmouth but Yarmouth is what the town is known by locally. And in a book of places listed alphabetically it's good to finish at the end (well nearly, none of them begin with a Z).

YARMOUTH OUTER HARBOUR
February 2010
What a difference a day makes!

YARMOUTH HARBOUR: CRUISE SHIP 'COLUMBUS'

June 2010 saw the first cruise ship enter the new outer harbour. The German operated 145-metre long charter ship *Columbus* carried one-hundred-and-ninety-five employees and clients from Germany to Norfolk for the opening ceremony of the Palm Paper plant at King's Lynn, along with forty commercial passengers.

YARMOUTH: TURBINES' MICROCLIMATE

Mike Page was intrigued by the mist which, in certain weather conditions, gathers round the wind turbines off Great Yarmouth. It seems that a microclimate happens when cold moist air from sea level is drawn towards colder air above the turbines creating a mist which shrouds the turbines themselves. In strong winds the mist disperses as it forms.

BIBLIOGRAPHY

ALDERTON & BOOKER, *Guide to the Industrial Archaeology of East Anglia*, Batsford 1980

CHADWICK Owen, *Victorian Miniature*, Futura 1983

CLARKE David, *The Country Houses of Norfolk*, Clarke 2006

COOK Olive, *Breckland*, Hale 1980

DAVISON Alan, *Deserted Villages in Norfolk*, Poppyland 1996

DUTT William, *Highways & Byways in East Anglia*, Jarrold 1914

DYMOND David, *The Norfolk Landscape*, Alastair Press 1990

EKWALL Eilert, *The Concise Oxford Dictionary of Place Names*, Clarendon Press 1977

HARROD Wilhemine, *The Norfolk Guide*, Alastair Press 1988

JENKINS Simon, *England's Thousand Best Churches*, Penguin 1999

KENNETT David H A, *Guide to the Norfolk Way*, Constable 1983

MEERES Frank, *Not of this World – Norfolk's Monastic Houses*, Meeres 2001

PEVSNER Nikolaus ,*The Buildings of England: North East Norfolk & Norwich*, Penguin 1976

PEVSNER Nikolaus, *The Buildings of England: North West & South Norfolk*, Penguin 1977

RAINBIRD CLARKE R, *East Anglia*, Thames & Hudson 1960

SKIPPER Keith, *Hidden Norfolk*, Countryside Books 1998

SMITH Graham, *Norfolk Airfields in the Second World War*, Countryside Books 1994

POCOCK Tom, *Norfolk*, Pimlico 1995

TOULSON Shirley, *East Anglia*, Whittett Books 1979

WILLIAMSON Tom, *England's Landscape – East Anglia*, Collins 2006

WINKLEY George, *The Country Houses of Norfolk*, Tyndale 1986